PURPOSE IS ABOUT DOING THE RIGHT THING
Purpose Letters Vol 2
A 30-Day Devotional

Dr Samuel Ekundayo

PURPOSE IS ABOUT DOING THE RIGHT THING

Copyright© 2025 | Dr Samuel Ekundayo

All rights reserved; no part of this publication may be reproduced, stored in a retrieval system or transmitted in any form or by any means electrical, mechanical, photocopying, recording or otherwise – without the prior written permission of the author or publisher.

The right of Dr Samuel Ekundayo to be identified as the author of this book has been asserted by him in

accordance with copyright laws.

ISBN: 978-1-7385992-6-4

For all information, address all correspondence to the author's website: www.samuelekundayo.com

DEDICATION

This book is dedicated to you dear reader. I pray that you will discover and fulfil the purpose of God for your life and be all He has created you to be in Jesus' name.

Amen!

I believe in you.

ACKNOWLEDGEMENTS

Firstly, I thank God for giving me the ability to write this book. Every opportunity to bless my generation through my writing give me so much fulfilment and I attribute that to the grace and gift of God.

To my Dudushewa and Treasure, I thank you for your consistent love, encouragement, and companionship. Thank you for believing in me and always rooting for me. I love you endlessly.

And to my parents (biological and spiritual), mentors and guides God has placed over me, thank you for all you have done and still doing to stir me in the right direction. I will always be grateful.

Special thanks to my team of amazing and God-sent individuals God has used for me to write this book. Pastor Ayodele Mike for your help in rewriting the initial parts of the book; Pastor Sam Adetiran for helping me edit the book, and my beloved Opeoluwa Adebakin for the beautifully designed book cover.

Table of Contents

Dedication 4

Acknowledgements 5

Day 1: Are You Doing The Right Thing? 8

Day 2: God Is A Rewarder 12

Day 3: Don't Be Frustrated When People Don't See Your Worth 16

Day 4: What Legacy Are You Living? 21

Day 5: The Power Of Knowledge 25

Day 6: Start Seeing Yourself As A Brand – 1 28

Day 7: Start Seeing Yourself As A Brand – 2 31

Day 8: Waiting Is Necessary 35

Day 9: Don't Be Like Alice In Alice's Adventures In Wonderland 39

Day 10: You Are A Product Of Relationships 43

Day 11: You Are Not A Loser 47

Day 12: You Can Do The Impossible 51

Day 13: God Is With You 55

Day 14: You Can Do Nothing Without The Holy Spirit 58

Day 15: What Are You Good At? 61

Day 16: Do You Have Fire In Your Belly? 65

Day 17: Beware Of Distractions 68

Day 18: Easy Things Can Become Difficult 71

Day 19: Consult The Word Daily 74

Day 20: You Have An Anointing 78

Day 21: Cursed Work Isn't What God
Has In Mind For You 81

Day 22: What Does Success Mean? 83

Day 23: You May Feel Unqualified 85

Day 24: God Wants To Use You. Yes, You! 88

Day 25: Lay Aside Every Weight 93

Day 26: Obscurity Is Not Always A Curse 98

Day 27: Find Your Domain 101

Day 28: Time Is Not Money 104

Day 29: Focus On Your Focus 107

Day 30: Who Is In Your Circle? 110

DAY 1

ARE YOU DOING THE RIGHT THING?

I was doing a paid clarity session for a client recently and he talked about how all his life, he'd just been doing good things but still felt empty on the inside.

He had been doing what many people would call 'great things,' yet God was nudging him that he wasn't fulfilling his purpose.

When he shared this with me, I understood because I've come to realise that purpose is not about doing good things, it's about doing the right thing.

So many people in the quest for success are just full of doing things because others around them are 'doing' things. Some are doing things they don't understand but because they see others doing those things, they also venture into them but are

PURPOSE IS ABOUT DOING THE RIGHT THING

now frustrated because they are not getting the same results those people are getting.

When it comes to purpose, the knowledge of your identity, the understanding of who you were created to be, and what you were made to do are more important than just doing anything that seems noble or good. This is why purpose has a lot to do with who you are becoming than what you are doing.

This reminds me of the time Jesus visited the house of two sisters – Mary and Martha (Luke 10:38 – 42). When Jesus got to their house, Martha, the elder sister, was full of zest and excitement. She was ostentatious in her gesture. She was all about ensuring Jesus had the kind of dinner they would be proud of. The Bible recorded that she was preparing a big dinner. Unfortunately for her, she was on the mission alone because Mary, her younger sister, had a different mindset. She was not about to miss a golden opportunity to glean all she could from the Lord Jesus. So, she chose to sit at His feet, listening and spending quality time with Him.

Martha, who was busy trying to impress Jesus all by herself, voiced out her frustration – "'...Lord, doesn't it seem unfair to you that my sister just sits here while I do all the work? Tell her to come and help me.'" (Luke 10:40 NLT). Jesus' response is worth meditating on. He said to Martha, 'but just one is needed. <u>Mary has chosen the right thing</u>, and it will not be taken away from her.' (Luke 10:42 GNT Emphasis Added). Mary knew and did the right thing. She was not moved by all

Martha was doing. She was not just trying to get things done like Martha. She found and focused on the right thing. Do not be moved by what others are doing. Find and focus on your right thing.

I also noticed that it didn't make sense to Martha that Mary was sitting at the feet of Jesus. Martha would rather Mary was with her in the kitchen doing things. But life is not about doing things, it's about doing the right thing. I love how Jeff Weiner puts it; he said, 'Execution is not just about getting things done, it's about getting the right things done.' It is dangerous to be getting things done at the expense of doing the right things.

I am sure you are already asking - how do I know my right thing? How do I know the right thing to do with my life? How do I escape the frustrating cycle of defective activities? How do I remain unbothered about what others are doing to focus on my right thing?

The answer is simple; like Mary, focus on Jesus! Focus on your Creator. Focus on God. Develop a relationship with Him and ask:, Lord, what would You have me do? What did You create me to do for You? What gifts have you given to me to fulfil your purpose?

God is so faithful. He will answer you. His answer will save you from the rat race of competing with other people or for the limelight. There is something about you that is so unique; it is not universal, and God wants to reveal it to you by His

Spirit. This is why the Bible says, '...No eye has seen, no ear has heard, and no mind has imagined what God has prepared for those who love him. But it was to us that God revealed these things by his Spirit. For his Spirit searches out everything and shows us God's deep secrets.' (1 Corinthians 2:9-10 NLT). To know your right thing, you have no choice but to have a relationship with the Holy Spirit. Only Him can reveal the mind of God to you, else you will just find yourself busy doing everything but the right thing.

Only the Holy Spirit can reveal your right thing to you.

I believe in you.

Day 2

GOD IS A REWARDER

I am a lecturer, and I often have to mark my students' reports. One of my mantras when marking is to reward hard working students based on the evidence presented in their work.

For instance, if I had marked a report of a student that fulfilled the requirements and hypothetically, I scored him 90%, and then I marked another student's whose work demonstrated greater evidence of hard work than the previous student, I am often more inclined to score the latter more than the former.

Why am I sharing this with you?

God is a rewarder. Although He doesn't reward the way man rewards, but He is a faithful and just rewarder. In fact, one of God's major attributes that we often forget is that He is a rewarder. The Scripture is littered with references to God as a rewarder.

I particularly like how the writer of the Book of Hebrews puts it, 'But without faith it is impossible to please Him, for he who comes to God must believe that He is, and that He is a rewarder of those who diligently seek Him.' (Hebrews 11:6 NKJV).

Simply put, if you have faith in God, and serve Him in obedience, He will reward you. The kingdom of God is not necessarily meritocratic; it is in the nature of God to reward faithfulness.

The Parable of talents (Matthew 25:14-30) references this nature of God to reward. The servants who came back with more talents were rewarded for their faithfulness, while the one who did nothing got nothing in return.

We were also told in Hebrews 10:35 not to 'cast away our confidence, which has great reward.' Who gives the reward for our confidence in Him? God!

To cap it all, in the Book of Revelation, God Himself declared, '...behold, I am coming quickly, and My reward is with Me, to give to every one according to his work.' (Revelation 22:12 NKJV).

God gives rewards and He is a rewarder. This means God rewards faithful, obedient, and hardworking children of His who when they hear His voice or instructions, do not turn away or turn deaf ears. The amazing fact is that God rewards both here on earth, and in eternity. This reminds me of Jesus' response to Peter in Matthew 19. Peter had asked Jesus what the reward for leaving everything behind to follow Him was.

Jesus responded, 'And anyone and everyone who has left houses or brothers or sisters or father or mother or children or lands for My name's sake will receive many [even a hundred] times more and will inherit eternal life.' (Matthew 19:29 AMPC).

The Bible also says that God has not called the house of Jacob to seek Him in vain (Isaiah 45:19).

God rewards and He rewards generously. Whatever God asks you to do, the best thing is to pay close attention and obey. That you obeyed God means you honoured Him; it means a lot to God when you are obedient to His instructions. Just think about it this way, you have a child who is always carrying out your instructions to the letter. The child will never disobey you for any reason. In fact, the child is always ready to go the extra mile just to make sure that your clear instructions are carried out. I know you would so much love this child and be willing to do anything and everything for them.

This was what happened to Abraham, God told him to leave his father's nation to another, and he obeyed without questioning God. This was why God so much loved Abraham and eventually made him father of many nations. You can note something with Abraham, God later rewarded him with Isaac. God doesn't despise people's obedience; He doesn't treat those who treat Him with honour like trash. He will always love and guard them. I just want to encourage you to do whatever God has been asking you to do; just do it, even if it is not convenient for you.

Has God told you to write a book? Then go ahead and write it! Your obedience has a reward. Has God told you to start a particular programme? Then start it today! Because your faithfulness to that vision has rewards. Whatever God has told you to do, if you obey, He will surely reward you generously. I challenge you to start doing whatever God has been asking you to start right away.

I believe in you.

DAY 3

DON'T BE FRUSTRATED WHEN PEOPLE DON'T SEE YOUR WORTH

I was studying my Bible lately, and I came across the story of Jesus visiting his hometown, Nazareth, where He grew up.

Let me put a few verses here for you to understand the context.

Matthew 13:54-58 (NLT):

'54 He returned to Nazareth, his hometown. When he taught there in the synagogue, everyone was amazed and said, "Where does he get this wisdom and the power to do miracles?" 55 Then they scoffed, "He's just the carpenter's son, and we know Mary, his mother, and his brothers—James, Joseph, Simon, and Judas. 56 All his sisters live right here among us. Where did he learn all these things?" 57 And they were deeply

PURPOSE IS ABOUT DOING THE RIGHT THING

offended and refused to believe in him. Then Jesus told them, "A prophet is honoured everywhere except in his own hometown and among his own family." 58 And so he did only a few miracles there because of their unbelief.'

See, when people are very familiar with your past, it's often only natural for them to disregard or take for granted your growth and the changes in your life.

These people were familiar with the young Jesus - the carpenter's son. They thought they had seen all of Him and all He could do. When He came back to town and started to preach and do miracles, they were not just amazed, they were offended.

Take note of the phrase, 'deeply offended.' It means, 'Who does he think He is? We know all His family members; we've known Him since He was a kid running around the streets in shorts; how dare He talk to us with such authority or do these great things as if He is something important...'

They were so offended that they refused to believe in Him or whatever He had to do in the town.

This has happened to me and is still happening to me.

It is very possible you are facing the same thing right now or will face it in your future, where the people around you appear not to value you or know your worth, whereas, the people who are not close to you are enjoying all of God's deposits on your inside, and you wish the people close to you would see it so they could tap from you.

The truth is, it is natural for them not to see your worth unless some of them are very intentional about it or God has spoken to them about you.

David had the potential of a king, yet his family members, including his Dad, didn't think much of him than for him to be at the backside of the desert tending sheep. Joseph was a great dreamer and interpreter of dreams, yet his brothers hated his guts. The Christian Jews didn't like the sight of Paul at all. Every time he came to town, they wanted to beat him up or stone him.

If this happens or is happening to you, don't let it get the best of you. Don't be frustrated. It's one of the strategies of the enemy to get you frustrated and angry and perhaps want to prove yourself to them.

Listen, you don't have to prove yourself to anyone. It is not your job to prove your worth, let God do it for you. If you are patient and focused on what God has called you to do, the anointing and grace in your life will speak for you eventually.

But for now, you must stay humble, hold your peace and keep doing what God has called you to do in the capacity He has called you to do it in the present. It will eventually be their loss because they will not be able to enjoy that grace in your life. Like the Bible recorded, Jesus was not able to do much there - 'He did only a few miracles there because of their unbelief.'

PURPOSE IS ABOUT DOING THE RIGHT THING

I also need to tell you to keep doping your best. Even if your best is never appreciated by those around you, keep doing it. Those who don't believe in you today will later come back to bow to you tomorrow. It happened to Joseph; his brothers never believed in him. In fact, they saw him as trash, if not they wouldn't have thrown him into the pit, or sold him as a slave into a strange land, and so on. If only they knew what this boy carried, they would have been treating him like a king right from when he was with them.

But do you know what's happening? A king will not always receive honour from his people because of over familiarity. If people don't also believe in what you carry because of over familiarity, don't lose focus, rather keep your eye on the goal, keep your eyes on the vision God has set before you. Stop seeking approval from anyone, stop seeking people's opinions. If Jesus was seeking approval that day, I am sure He won't go about His Father's business. But He rather focused and fixed His eyes on the assignment His Father placed before Him.

Let me tell you this, people did not call you, so no one has the obligation to discourage you from doing what God has sent you to do. One of the challenges with so many people is the need for acceptance; once they are not accepted, they will automatically think they are not called to do what they have been called to do. No, don't live your life that way! Whether they accept you or not, do what God has called you to do; whether you are celebrated or not, just do it, keep on moving,

PURPOSE IS ABOUT DOING THE RIGHT THING

one day those who are despising you today will be the same people that will come around to celebrate you.

Stay focused. Stay humble. Let God prove Himself through you and never try to prove a point to anyone.

I believe in you.

DAY 4

WHAT LEGACY ARE YOU LIVING?

There was a woman in the Bible, her name was not mentioned much; just a few verses were dedicated to her story. Her name was Tabitha, aka Dorcas. Her story was documented in Acts 9:36-43.

The Bible described her as a woman 'full of good works and charitable deeds.' Bear in mind, she was not an apostle or pastor, she was just a disciple. Her impact was so massive that when she fell sick and died, people could not bear the thought of her death. When Peter went to her place, the Bible recorded that 'all the widows stood by him (Peter) weeping, showing the tunics and garments which Dorcas had made while she was with them'

Needless to say that the woman was raised from the dead but that's not what I want to draw your attention to. I want to talk about her impact on others.

Without being unnecessarily morbid, God forbid you died today, what would others say about you?

What impact would they say you have made on their lives?

How would they say you have touched or added value to them?

Would they have stories of your significance or that of your significant troubles?

The worst way to live life as a child of God is to live it indifferently.

The worst way to live life as a child of God is for your impact not to be felt in your community.

The worst way to live life as a child of God is for you to die, and people have nothing to say about your value in their lives.

The worst way to live life as a child of God is for people to have no reason to want to pray to God to ask for you to be raised back to life.

Tabitha lived an exemplary life and thank God her story was documented for us.

Whether you like it not, your daily life is the legacy you are living and that you will leave behind. My advice is, you must make it count. Make it count in the kingdom of God, in your community, and in the world at large.

We do not have to wait till we're old to start living our legacy. You can begin to live a life of legacy from now onward. You are not too small to start it, and you are not too old to start either. You are born to make a difference, you are born to make things happen, just make sure your life is counting.

Meanwhile, I've seen some people make the mistake of saying they do not have anything, so that's why they are not living a life of impact and legacy. No, you don't need to have everything! What you have right now is able to make things happen. Your talent, potential, or special ability can go a long way in making your life and that of others around you better. Start with what you have, encourage someone, and give counsel to someone. You have more than three pairs of shoes, can you give a pair to someone who has only one? Yes, that's how to do it.

You don't even need to have all the world before you do something for someone, your words of counsel and encouragement can bring someone out of depression, your little hand of help can make another person's day. As you are reading this book now, there is something you can do that others around you cannot do, why not teach them how to do it?

Stop living a selfish life, it won't lead you anywhere. Just assume Dorcas was a selfish or self-centred woman, no one

PURPOSE IS ABOUT DOING THE RIGHT THING

would be there to stand for her when she died, but Peter was able to raise her back to life because of her good deeds.

Have you written one or two books? Why not give one or two out of the two books today to encourage someone?

Make every day of your life count, don't just exist or live for living sake, rather live for impact making; your life and future depends on it.

Now is the time to begin to live for what we want to be remembered for, and you do not have to be an apostle or pastor to do that, all you need is to be you and you are good to go.

I believe in you.

Day 5
THE POWER OF KNOWLEDGE

Recently, one of my fathers in faith came to our house. He saw the large paintings we had on our wall, and I noticed he was looking at them keenly. Staring at one of them for long, he queried, 'Where did you buy this - it must be expensive?'

'It's not too expensive sir,' I replied.

He said, this is a unique painting as compared to this other one (pointing at another one).

You can see it's unique because the brush strokes are visible and conspicuous, not only that, but the artist also signed it whereas the other one was not signed and there were no visible brush strokes.

PURPOSE IS ABOUT DOING THE RIGHT THING

I took my mind back to when we bought the painting, and realised that the unique one was truly the more expensive one.

He then said to me, 'Should the artist ever become famous, you could resell this for millions of dollars because it's a unique work of an artist; it was not mass-produced like the other one.'

You see, up until this lesson, I had no idea of the value of the paintings. My knowledge about them was zero, other than the fact that my wife and I love to have large paintings in our house, so we bought good ones.

Why am I sharing this with you?

Knowledge is the key to value.

Ever since that lecture about those wall arts, I have begun to look at them differently. In fact, I am starting to place more value on them, especially the unique one .

This is what I am trying to tell you: What you don't know anything about, you cannot truly value.

This reminds me of when Jesus met that woman at the well in John 4. Jesus said to her, '...If you only knew the gift God has for you and who you are speaking to, you would ask me, and I would give you living water.' (John 4:10 NKJV).

In other words, Jesus was saying, 'If you have any idea who I am, you will place greater value on my person and this conversation we're having.' Needless to say that the woman later got to know Jesus and valued Him but until then, she thought she was talking to just another Jewish man.

For everything a man would do and become, knowledge is key. If you don't have much knowledge about what you carry, you will not value yourself. This is why lots of people don't value themselves; they want to settle for what is not best, they want to settle for a low-quality living, they want to settle for a mediocre life.

Knowledge is the bedrock of value. In other words, if you don't have knowledge about your person and about who you are, you won't have respect for yourself and when you have lost respect for yourself, you won't value yourself anymore. Don't be ignorant of your person, know who you are and live a valuable life.

The moment Joseph interpreted dreams in the palace, he became a person of honor. Even before then, he had a keen knowledge of who he was, so he was always careful about the choices he made. He wouldn't settle to sleep with Potiphar's wife because of the value he placed upon his own life. Place value on yours too, know who you are, and live the kind of life God wanted you to live.

My prayer is that God will reveal yourself to you enough for you to know your true value and worth, such that in any area of your life where you may be doubting yourself and perhaps your confidence is low, you will start to carry yourself differently.

I believe in you.

DAY 6

START SEEING YOURSELF AS A BRAND – 1

If you understand God's purpose for your life, you will realise that you are a brand.

When we talk about branding, people always immediately think of companies and corporate organisations.

That was ages ago. Today, everyone is a brand and everything you do, whether consciously or unconsciously, creates and maintains your brand. Some people are known to rant on social media, what they fail to realise is that they are creating and maintaining the brand of a complainer or critic.

Wise people are always conscious of this and so they consciously and intentionally create their brand. This is so important because the world will largely accept you at the estimation of yourself. So, if you act, walk, talk like someone with no value, then you will be accepted that way.

I was reading an article online the other day and the author said, 'The question is no longer if you have a personal brand, but if you choose to guide and cultivate the brand or to let it be defined on your behalf.'

Some years ago, I started to coach my wife on how she could brand herself in relation to her purpose. On one of such occasions, I called her a Relationship Coach. My wife said, 'But I am not certified yet.' I told her that she doesn't need to be certified to begin to brand herself as one. If you immerse yourself in the subject or niche and you intentionally create a brand, the world will accept your brand. If you're reading this, I am passing the same message to you. I am asking you a question you must always ask yourself; what brand am I creating? Remember, consciously or unconsciously, you are creating a brand.

The key is to consciously create a brand that depicts value; a brand that's worth people's time and money.

The internet - particularly your social media - is a powerhouse for brand creation and maintenance. If you want to be seen as a preacher, stop posting about politics all the time. If you want to be seen as a mentor to the youth, stop talking bad about them. If you want to be seen as a motivational speaker, stop complaining and ranting on your Facebook page, TikTok,

Twitter/X or Instagram. If you don't stop, that brand you want to create for yourself will never see the light of day.

This reminds me of what the brothers of Jesus once said to him, 'For no one works in secret if he seeks to be known openly. If you do these things, show yourself to the world.' - John 7:4 ESV.

Whereas Jesus responded that his time had not yet come but he didn't dispute the truth in what they said.

If your time of manifestation is here, and you have a message, then you must begin to create your brand intentionally. Remember, 'You are the light of the world. A town built on a hill cannot be hidden' - Matthew 5:14 NIV.

Allow me to leave you with this. To create an effective brand, you must do something every day about that brand you're creating, and the world would soon notice you. In other words, you must be consistent.

Consistency establishes your reputation. If you want to be known, you must consistently share your message. If you don't consistently share what you know, then nobody will know you for what you know how to do. If you are given a mandate, then step into your mandate, start doing what God has called and ordained you to be.

I believe in you.

Day 7

START SEEING YOURSELF AS A BRAND – 2

Yesterday, I shared with you that consciously or unconsciously you are creating a brand. In other words, whether you like it or not, you are creating a brand. And the world will largely accept the estimation of yourself.

Today, I want to share with you what I call the power of a niche. See, there are too many 'general' people in the world today. To stand out, you must cease being general, and to stand out, you have to create what I call a niche.

In the words of the late Zig Ziglar, 'The great majority of people are "wandering generalities" rather than "meaningful specifics."'

One of the key ways to brand yourself is to be specific about your brand. Be a meaningful specific, not a wandering generality. You don't need to do what the general people or the masses are doing. One of the best ways you can continue to be living an abusive life is to keep doing what the general people are doing. If you want to be greater than what you are right now, then it is important that you don't try to do many things at a time, just pick something and build a niche around it.

How do you do this?

1. Ask yourself: What do I want to be known for? If you have noticed, general things rarely command value. It is the things that are rare that have great worth. People pay more for things that are rare. Rarity suggests significance and significance begets influence.

2. Ask yourself: What is one thing people think about when they mention my name or when people mention my name, what is that one thing that comes to their mind?

If people think about nothing when your name is mentioned, then your brand has no value yet. There is still a lot of work to do. People need to know you for something, you need to be deliberate about making people know who you are. If you don't give people the chance to know who you are, then you will keep shortchanging your sphere of influence because people won't be able to call or invite you to solve a particular problem for them.

Establish yourself in a niche; a niche where you have mastery and if you don't yet have mastery, then be determined to build it. You can start building your niche even as you are reading through this book now. Just think about it right and switch instantly, it only takes you to make one good decision that will change and transform your life totally. Make that decision today, decide on what you want to do with your life and move.

Having a niche helps your focus. And this invariably helps you to be consistent and persistent because you are not 'encumbered by too many things,' if I may borrow the words of Jesus in Luke 10:41.

You must immerse yourself in this niche till you cannot be ignored. Study all that is available on that subject, niche, or area; know all there is to know. Buy books, attend seminars, get certified, pay for coaching or mentorship, educate yourself and invest in personal development. This is where I have challenges with people. A lot of people really want to earn, but they are not ready and willing to learn. A lot of people still do not want to pay for coaching or mentorship programmes, they want it to be free. Free things don't last longer, if you really want to get serious about your life, then you must take things seriously. Sign up for a course, register for a mentorship programme, just do what will make people start perceiving this sign of seriousness in you. As you do that, with time, people will get adjusted to the new you.

Refuse mediocrity at all costs. No one pays a premium for mediocrity. Even if they do, as soon as they realise you lack depth or value, they either ask for a refund or bid your brand goodbye.

For example, my niche is purpose. This is an area I have immersed myself in for years. I have read a lot of books on the subject and still reading so much that even when I carry my Bible to read, purpose never fails to jump out at me. Immersion! This is why I have retained the name, 'The Purpose Preacher.'

My vision is that all over the world, when you mention purpose, you must mention Dr Samuel Ekundayo, the Purpose Preacher.

What is your vision for your brand? I hope this inspires you.

I believe in you.

Day 8

WAITING IS NECESSARY

My wife and I visited a restaurant recently for brunch. When we got there, we met some people who had already ordered their food and were waiting.

We took note of how long we'd have to wait for our food. After we ordered, we noticed a few people had their food delivered but there was a couple who didn't get theirs. Interestingly, our food came before theirs. They had to wait longer.

You see, we ordered pancakes and French toast, which I assume were easier to make for the chef.

A few minutes later, my wife called my attention to a long wooden platter being carried with all forms of delicacies. It was more than just one food on the platter. It seems they had ordered all sorts delivered so ravishingly on the long wooden platter.

On sighting the beautiful platter, everyone in the restaurant almost all echoed, 'Wow!' at the same time because it was a magnificent sight to behold. Immediately, my wife said, 'That's a great lesson right there.'

Nothing 'Wow!' comes quick. Nothing great happens quickly. Waiting is necessary for your destiny. Sometimes, it appears God is taking longer than usual.

You look around and it appears everyone else has had their prayers answered but you. You look at your neighbour's barns, and it seems full, whereas there is nothing yet to sight in yours. Your friends' quivers are full but yours look empty. Others seem to be enjoying blessings but for you, there is nothing to enjoy.

Listen, what God is preparing for you cannot be compared to your neighbour's. I'll never forget a statement I heard since I was a teenager, When God appears to be coming late, He is coming in a big way!'

The waiting process is God's system to either prepare us for what He is bringing our way or prepare what He is bringing our way for us. This is why waiting is necessary for your destiny. If you quit because you are impatient or think God is not fair, you will miss your blessing.

By the way, God is not a fair God. Instead, He is a just God. God doesn't do fairness - If God is a fair God, you would have everything your neighbours have or get married at the same time your age mates get married. God would not do things for you because He did the same for your friends or neighbors, He would rather do things for you that will bring glory to His name. I just want you to realise that God has not forgotten you. In fact, God doesn't forget anyone. God will always be judged faithful and at the right time and season, He will do what He has promised to do in your life.

God is faithful always, and He won't give you things because you are feeling bad. God doesn't work with emotions. He apportions to every one of us uniquely according to His purpose for our lives. Then, you also need to understand that God knows everyone's capacity and He understands what we can bear as a result. He wouldn't put on you, for instance, 50 thousand weights of glory if He knows that you can only bear the weight of 20 thousand.

This is why it is rather better to wait for God so He can make you more mature so as to bear the weight of glory He is preparing you for. Don't be in a hurry and don't rush out of your cooking season. Wait on God, allow Him to finish cooking you. Don't be impatient with God. Trust His leading. If He seems to be coming late, always remember, He is coming in a big way.

God can be trusted with your future.
God can be trusted with your destiny.
God can be trusted with your visions, dreams, and goals.
He will not disappoint, and He is never late. Trust His timing.

Trust Him with your vision, your dream and every aspirations of your life. Don't allow what's not working today to get you discouraged. Don't allow your present circumstances push you out of God's timing and mandate. Stay with God and stay on course. One day you will also be known like others, you will be blessed as others, you will have more resources like others; just be patient and allow God Himself to bring you into the season He is preparing for you.

I believe in you.

DAY 9

DON'T BE LIKE ALICE IN ALICE'S ADVENTURES IN WONDERLAND

Have you seen the movie, Alice's Adventures in Wonderland? In the movie, the main character, Alice, asked Cheshire Cat, 'Would you please tell me which way I ought to go from here?'

The Cat said, 'That depends a good deal on where you want to get to.' 'I don't care much where,' Alice replied. 'Then it doesn't matter which way you go,' the Cat responded.

The Cat was right. If you don't know where you are headed in life, then, everywhere and anywhere can be your destination.

This is why one of the greatest gifts God gave to mankind is the gift of vision. No wonder Dr Myles Munroe once said,

PURPOSE IS ABOUT DOING THE RIGHT THING

'The poorest man in the world is a man without a dream.' God wants to show you where He is taking you. God will never create anyone without filling them with something. There must be something you are born to do and be; you must be aspiring to be something.

It doesn't matter where you are coming from, God has a vision for your life. Joseph had a dream and regardless of those difficulties he went through, he never allowed them to dictate what his life will eventually amount to. The truth is, if Joseph didn't know where he was going, his challenges would have acted as an obstacle and would have stopped him from going to the place God was taking him.

'That she caught him by his garment, saying, "Lie with me." But he left his garment in her hand and fled and ran outside.' Genesis 39:12 NKJV.

Check the above scripture again, Joseph could have lied with Potiphar's wife, thinking that would be the way out of his slavery. But he rather ran away. Let me tell you, you must do everything in your capacity to walk through the route God is taking you, don't deviate from the call and mandate for your life. Don't allow your vision to go against God's vision and will for your life. God has a better vision for you. Joseph could have seen an option of escape by sleeping with Potiphar's wife, but he knew God had better plans and vision for him, so he held on to what God had for him.

PURPOSE IS ABOUT DOING THE RIGHT THING

He is a God of vision, and He delights in revealing the future to His children. He once told Abraham, '...Look as far as you can see in every direction—north and south, east and west. I am giving all this land, as far as you can see, to you and your descendants as a permanent possession.' Genesis 13:14-15 NLT.

Let me ask you this important question: How far can you see? God wants to do much more for you and the children He has given or will give you. If all you see about you are all you can see with your physical eyes, you need to look again. There are realms of the unseen God wants you to tap into. The physical sight is a major enemy of God's vision for your life, so you must learn to look with your spiritual eyes such that if physically you can see defeat, in the spiritual you would be seeing victory.

Jesus got to the tomb of Lazarus. Everyone there had given up hope.

Jesus got there, and said, 'He is asleep.' He saw differently. In Jesus' account, He was already seeing a resurrected Lazarus.

Vision is the source of hope and the foundation for a great future. Vision will enable you to see greatness in the seed God has sown inside of you even when nobody is seeing it. You can be sure that the future is sure and certain for you if you have a great vision in what you are doing even when others are not seeing it. Vision will keep you on the right track. If you want to go amiss, vision will enable you to see and follow the right path, even when no one seems to see a big deal about what you are doing. Let me tell you this, if nobody has hope in you, God has hope in you and you must also have hope in yourself. If your own hope never dies, then God will never stop doing something great in your life.

No wonder God said, *'Where there is no vision, the people perish...'*
Proverbs 29:18a KJV.

If you are yet to see anything about your future through your spiritual eyes, I want to give you a prayer point that I recommend you pray regularly. Always pray, 'Lord, show me where You are taking me.'

I've been praying this prayer for years now and it's amazing what God has been showing me about my future. I can never be hopeless. There are so many things God has shown me that I am yet to see come to pass and I look forward to them, so I am full of hope and excitement about the future.

I know what the future holds because God has shown me.

You too can know what your future holds such that even amidst despair and storms, you are confident and assured. Don't give up on your dream. If Joseph could refuse to give up, then you should just keep moving on as well because one day your dreams will eventually become a reality.

I believe in you.

Day 10
YOU ARE A PRODUCT OF RELATIONSHIPS

I am a product of relationships, and I will always be grateful for the relationships I have in my life; from my relationship with my wife and children, to close friends, mentors, proteges and my outer circle of friends. One day, I sat down and looked through some of the major events in my life, and realised God used relationships to make them happen.

For instance:

I met my wife through a friend.

I got my first university admission through the help of a senior colleague.

I am in New Zealand today because of my dad's friend.

God took our family to Singapore through relationships.

My fees for undergraduate and postgraduate studies were paid through relationships.

We bought our first house in New Zealand through our mentor.

My Pastor helped me to purchase my very first car.

I got my first full-time job in New Zealand through relationships

Can you see that I am a product of relationships?

You are too. You may not admit it, but you are.

No wonder someone claimed that 80% of your success in life is determined by your relationships; only 20% is determined by your solo effort. You would agree with me that 80% is a lot. Therefore, I submit to you that the quality of your relationships determines the quality of your life.

Whenever I talk about relationships, I am reminded of what one of my mentors, Bishop Bob Alonge, taught me some years ago.

In his book, THE MAKING OF A CHOSEN VESSEL, he said, 'Your life as a chosen vessel consists of two groups of people – Your Crowd and your company.'

For instance, Jesus chose twelve TO BE WITH HIM – He was not always with everybody. He didn't commit to everyone in equal dimensions. Simply put, your company is your team, and your crowd are just your beneficiaries.

PURPOSE IS ABOUT DOING THE RIGHT THING

Let me help you with 7 core differences between your company and the crowd:

- The crowd will drain you, but your company will lift you.
- The crowd will crucify you, but your company will carry your cross for you.
- The crowd will increase your fear, but your company will increase your faith.
- The crowd will eventually turn against you, but your company will always be there to hold your hand.
- The crowd will amplify your weakness, but your company will amplify your strengths.
- The crowd will corrupt you, but your company will help you unlock and maximise your (hidden) potential.
- The crowd will try to compete with you, but your company is committed to your growth.

Now, let me tell you this, inasmuch as the relationship you keep will be a plus to you and they have a lot to do with your growth (and if you keep the right relationship, you will definitely grow), you must also be committed to making them grow. As you are getting benefits from your friends, relatives, colleagues or probably your family members, make sure they are also getting benefits through you; make sure they are growing in their company with you.

PURPOSE IS ABOUT DOING THE RIGHT THING

That's how a good and sound relationship works, when you receive, you will also give in return. Give and take makes relationships work better; if you are always on the receiving end, that relationship may collapse one day and you may be left alone. Build good relationships, and nurture them with everything you have.

I hope this has helped you.

I believe in you.

Day 11

YOU ARE NOT A LOSER

I was taking my boys to their football game one Saturday morning when I asked both of them to pray for us. The eldest, Semiloore, prayed followed by Feranmi, his brother. Feranmi made a statement in his prayer that I still find very powerful. He said, 'Lord, if we lose today, help us to remember that we are not losers.'

When he was done praying, I asked him where he heard the statement from, and he said, from no one. What a mindset!

What's so powerful about that prayer is that Feranmi has learnt to separate his identity from life events.

If you are going to effectively fulfil God's purpose for your life, you must not let life situations and circumstances determine your identity. Hence, you must start realising that even if you fail, you are not a failure; that even if you make mistakes, you are not a mistake.

Your identity is far superior, bigger, and greater than whatever happens or does not happen to you. Which means you are not the result of your mistakes or errors, you are made for more. Mistake is not your identity, failure is not your destination in life; it is a journey and a process, and if you have not given up on yourself, you will get to the place God has destined you to be.

Your identity is powerful, and it is what makes the whole of you, if you lose it to a mere event that happens to you, then you may not get it again on a platter of gold. Do everything to protect your identity; you were made by the Almighty God to do mighty works, so even if you get to a point where it seems you are failing and nothing seems to be working, you will always remember that you were made by the Almighty God in His mighty image.

Where your identity is concerned, it is crucial that you know that you were made in the image of God, and you carry His nature. You carry upon yourself the identity of God; the moment you realise this truth, then nothing will move you again. Don't lose your identity to failure, rather lose errors or mistakes you have once made in your life. Those things don't define your personality, they are just normal events that are bound to happen to people. If you allow your failures to get at

PURPOSE IS ABOUT DOING THE RIGHT THING

you, then you may have to pay dearly for your negligence. But can I tell you this? 'Don't ever allow your failure to get at you.'

Don't let the storms tell you anything different. Don't let the valley seasons you go through make you feel any less. Don't let the mistakes you make in life tell you anything different.

'I said, "You are god's, And all of you are children of the Most High."' Psalms 82:6 NKJV.

Have you seen your reality in the Scripture? Even God says that you are a god too, so why are you looking down on yourself because you did or tried something and you failed. You are not the first person that will have that kind of experience, and you will never be the last. People failed yesterday, some people are failing as you are reading this book, more people will still fail tomorrow and years to come.

So listen to me, you are not your mistakes. You are not your failures. You are who God says you are. You are not your errors, you are a god. You are not your failures, you are a god. You are God's masterpiece, and He made you beautifully in His own very image and likeness.

You are chosen.
You are royal.
You are a priest.
You are loved.

Any time the devil tries to rub your failures in your face, remind him that '...you are a chosen generation, a royal

PURPOSE IS ABOUT DOING THE RIGHT THING

priesthood, a holy nation, His own special people, that you may proclaim the praises of Him who called you out of darkness into His marvelous light.' - 1 Peter 2:9 NKJV.

I believe in you.

DAY 12
YOU CAN DO THE IMPOSSIBLE

I had just completed my bachelor's degree in a private school in Singapore. It's one of those schools with affiliation to universities overseas. Interestingly, before I joined the school, and in their years of existence, no students have ever crossed over from that school to the top universities in Singapore to further their studies.

I think many of the students were just too timid to make the application or didn't have the kind of rugged vision or faith I had.

I was different. I came to the school with a vision to go for my master's degree as soon as I completed my bachelor's degree.

I didn't care about history or precedence, I just applied. You guessed right, I got the admission.

The best part is that I got two admissions into the top two universities in Singapore. I had to sit down to choose which of them I wanted to attend.

Needless to say that I became the poster boy for the school. I was being used as an advertisement to say subsequent students could now apply to the top universities in Singapore which were amongst the top 100 universities in the world.

Why am I sharing this with you?

You too can do the impossible. With your God, all things are possible. I don't know what you are believing in God for right now that seems impossible, I dare you to believe in God, and take a step of faith today.

Yes, make that application.
Yes, make that appointment.
Visit that scholarship website today.
Make that call right now.
Just step up and step out in faith!

This reminds me of how Peter stepped out of the boat the other day. He said, '"Lord, if it's you," Peter replied, "tell me to come to you on the water"' - Matthew 14:28 NIV.

Jesus did not deny him. Jesus simply said, 'Come!' What happened next defied all natural laws. This had never happened before in the history of time, but Peter broke the record, he did the impossible, he walked on the water, none of the other disciples did it again and no one else has from that time till tomorrow. You can also break records; you too can do what others have not done before. You can go where any of your family members have not gone before. You can achieve what any of your family members have not achieved before. Just go out there and do it!

I mean, we knew Jesus was superhuman, but Peter was as human as we all. He made history. It was recorded that, 'He got down out of the boat, walked on the water and came toward Jesus.' (Matthew 14:29 NIV). You too can make history; you can make a story and make a difference.

Wow! If we dare believe the Word of God, we too can do the impossible. In fact, when Jesus was about to go, He told His disciples something, note what He told them:

'Most assuredly, I say to you, he who believes in Me, the works that I do he will do also; and greater works than these he will do, because I go to My Father.'
John 14:12 NKJV.

Have you read for yourself what Jesus told His disciples? He wasn't just talking to His disciples, He was also talking to you, you can do greater works than Jesus did, yes you can!

Amazingly, Jesus Himself says, "...all things are possible to him who believes"? - Mark 9:23 NKJV.

Do you believe it? If truly you believe it, just begin to see yourself as the person doing greater things, believe in yourself and believe you have the capacity to do it. As you take a step

PURPOSE IS ABOUT DOING THE RIGHT THING

of faith this day, God will go before you and make all crooked paths straight, in Jesus' name.

I believe in you.

DAY 13

GOD IS WITH YOU

One day, a young man looked at me and said, 'You have such a perfect life, and everything is working for you.'

Amused, I laughed. I told him that what he sees about me now is not how it has always been. I've been through a lot to be where I am, and while everything now seems perfect, the real secret is that God has been there for me and still is. If we are going to fulfil our life's purpose, one of our strongest convictions must be that God is with us.

Nicodemus, a Pharisee, went to Jesus one night, when no one would notice him, and said these exact words to Jesus, 'Rabbi, we know that you are a teacher who has come from God. For no one could perform the signs you are doing if God were not with him.' - John 3:2 NIV.

Jesus was an undeniable expression of signs and wonders because God was with Him, and people, including those who did not like him, noticed.

All through Joseph's turmoil, from the pit, to slavery, to Potiphar's house, to the prison and eventually the palace, five good times, the Bible recorded, 'But the Lord was with Joseph.'

What a testimony!

See, we cannot do anything great if God is not with us. Do you know another shocking fact? God is with you! If God's not with you, you wouldn't be where you are today, it is the evidence that God is truly with you. Now, this is what I want to tell you, the fact that God is with you means you will do greater things.

You are never walking alone, like the Liverpool Football Club slogan says, 'You'll Never Walk alone.' If you are walking through the darkest moment of your life, God is with you. If you are down and nothing seems to be working for you, God is still with you.

'The LORD of hosts is with us; The God of Jacob is our refuge.' Psalms 46:11 NKJV.

The above scripture is evidence that God is with you, if He can be with Joseph when he was thrown into the pit, if He was with him when he was thrown into the prison, then He is with you as well. Don't assume anything less.

PURPOSE IS ABOUT DOING THE RIGHT THING

Today, I just want to challenge you to remain solid in your conviction that God is with you. Your conviction about Him being with you will bring confidence to your heart and will help you to keep moving on.

In His words, '...I will never leave you nor forsake you.' - Hebrews 13:5 NKJV.

This is also my conviction.

I believe in you.

Day 14
YOU CAN DO NOTHING WITHOUT THE HOLY SPIRIT

There was a time in my life where I took time to learn about the Holy Spirit. One of my discoveries was that the Holy Spirit is the Father of the New Creation. In other words, we are in the dispensation of the Holy Spirit.

Jesus died, resurrected and went back to heaven but in His words, 'And I will pray the Father, and he shall give you another Comforter, that He may abide with you forever.' John 14:16 KJV.

The Holy Spirit is that comforter that abides with us forever.

Jesus was born by the Holy Spirit (Matthew 1:18), did all He did through the Holy Spirit (Acts 10:38), and resurrected by the Holy Spirit (Romans 8:11).

So, we too are nothing without the Holy Spirit.

Why am I sharing this with you?

Your purpose on earth cannot be fulfilled without a genuine fellowship with the person of the Holy Spirit. You must be intentional about building an intimate relationship with the Holy Spirit because He is ready to build one with you.

You must be totally dependent on Him for you to fully realise your potential and be all that God has created you to be. Without the power of the Holy Spirit upon you, you will remain northing and empty. The Apostles did everything they did by the Holy Spirit, and in the very beginning of their ministries, Jesus had an instruction for them, 'And being assembled together with them, He commanded them not to depart from Jerusalem, but to wait for the Promise of the Father, "which," He said, "you have heard from Me;' - Acts 1:4 NKJV.

The Holy Spirit is not just a symbol, but a person and He desires us to have fellowship with Him. This is why Paul, by revelation knowledge, declared in 2 Corinthians 13:14 NKJV - ' The grace of the Lord Jesus Christ, the love of God, and the fellowship of the Holy Spirit be with you all. Amen.'

Jesus gives grace, God gives love, but the Holy Spirit demands fellowship. The word fellowship there is the word 'koinonia' which translates as 'intercourse.'

The Holy Spirit wants us to have a close and intimate fellowship with Him more than a man has with his wife. He wants to be our closest partner and friend. The Holy Spirit wants us to depend on Him for everything.

If we fellowship with the Holy Spirit intimately, like Jesus, nothing will be impossible for us because with Him in us we can do all things. So, let me ask you today - How dependent are you on the Holy Spirit?

I believe in you.

Day 15

WHAT ARE YOU GOOD AT?

Some years ago, I was talking to my Dad on the phone and I said to him, 'Dad, I think I knew why we were poor when I was younger.' 'Why?' my Dad asked. I said, 'It's because people didn't know what to come to us for.'

You see, no one was created poor. Though we were created naked, we were not created empty. We all came to the earth with a gift or talent of some sort that we didn't learn from anywhere. One of the issues with many people is that they are yet to discover that thing, so no one is seeking them for it.

Your gift is God's gift to you, and what you do with it is your gift to the world. You were given the gift to make the world a better place, and to bring God glory. God is glorified when we are doing what we've been created to do.

This reminds me of the scripture that says, 'Thou art worthy, O Lord, to receive glory and honour and power: for thou hast created all things, and for thy pleasure they are and were created.' - Revelations 4:11 KJV.

We were created for God's pleasure, and we bring Him pleasure when He watches us do the very things He created us to do. Remember, Ephesians 2:10 NLT says, 'For we are God's masterpiece. He has created us anew in Christ Jesus, so we can do the good things he planned for us long ago.'

There is something God created us to do a very long time ago and we have been empowered to do them through the gifts and talents deposited inside of us. It is when you develop mastery of your gifts that you become sought-after. No one becomes known for doing nothing, you will become known for what you do. With this, I can boldly tell you that you were not created to be poor. You shouldn't be poor because everything you need to come out of poverty has been created into you by God.

People will look for you for what you are carrying but they won't look for you if you let it lie dormant within you. They won't look for you if you don't refine your gifts. Most of the influential people you see out there are people who carry one or two potentials. You also have a potential, there is something in you, it is lying low inside of you because you are not making use of it; it is remaining dormant in you because you don't even know you have it. It is amazing to know that so many people

PURPOSE IS ABOUT DOING THE RIGHT THING

are so talented, but without any impact on the surface of the earth. Well, it is not their fault, it is because most of those people never understand what it means to discover oneself.

But the fact that you are reading this book right now means you understood what it means to discover oneself. It is important that you discover what you can do because this will give you privileges and will open doors of opportunities for you.

David knew he could fight Goliath when the opportunity came for him, but before that time, he had discovered that he was strong and could fight because he had been fighting wild animals in the forest. He understood what he could do and this brought him an opportunity which he maximised.

David was in the back side of the desert, facing lions and bears every day, seemingly rejected and abandoned until someone told the king, 'I have seen a son of Jesse of Bethlehem who knows how to play the harp. He is a mighty man of valour, a warrior, eloquent and handsome, and the LORD is with him.' - 1 Samuel 16:18 BSB.

When people see you, what do they see? Do they see your gifts at work? Even more importantly, are you aware of your gifts? Are you adding value daily to people with your gifts? Are you refining your gifts through education, practice and consistency?

This is what makes the world look for you.

Joseph was in Prison when the Butler told the king (Pharaoh) that 'Now there was a young Hebrew man with us there, a servant of the captain of the guard. And we told him, and he interpreted our dreams for us; to each man he interpreted according to his own dream. And it came to pass, just as he interpreted for us, so it happened. He restored me to my office, and he hanged him.' - Genesis 41:12-13 NKJV.

What are your gifts? Never forget that your gifts are the source of the light that you are to the world and the flavour that makes you the salt of the earth. Without your gift, you would die ordinary. God wants you to affect the world and cause a dent in it with your gifts. It is time to arise and shine for your light has come, so gentiles can come to your light, and kings to the brightness of your rising.

If you believe it, say 'AMEN' wherever you are.

I believe in you.

DAY 16

DO YOU HAVE FIRE IN YOUR BELLY?

I want to show you another scripture that challenges me from time to time. They are the echoes of Prophet Jeremiah, and they read thus.

'But if I say, "Forget it! No more God-Messages from me!" The words are fire in my belly, burning in my bones. I'm worn out trying to hold it in. I can't do it any longer!' - Jeremiah 20:9 MSG.

Have you ever mistakenly drunk or sipped hot coffee or tea before? It's either you gulped it down in horror or spit it out as quickly as you can.

Fire burns! And Prophet Jeremiah refers to God's words in his belly as fire. In his words, 'I'm worn out trying to hold it in. I can't do it any longer.' I make bold to say, if you have found

God's purpose for your life, it comes with an unquenchable fire and hunger to pursue it. If you can't feel this passion, it is worth crying to God about.

We all must sound like Apostle Paul when he said, 'But my life is worth nothing to me unless I use it for finishing the work assigned me by the Lord Jesus—the work of telling others the Good News about the wonderful grace of God.' - Acts 20:24 NLT.

The same Apostle Paul said, 'For though I preach the gospel, I have nothing to glory of: for necessity is laid upon me; yea, woe is unto me, if I preach not the gospel!' - 1 Corinthians 9:16 KJV.

What passion!
What fire!
What hunger!

We all must come to this place where life is worth nothing unless we're all about the purpose of God for our lives. Not another big house, or car, or job, or accolade.

Our lives must be such that we're daily living for the approval of one - Our God Almighty!

I am writing to ask you in today's letter - do you have fire in your belly?

Do you have a burden for God's purpose that has engulfed your entire life and existence that nothing else matters other than bringing God glory and pleasing Him with your life? A passion must be burning inside of you, you must be on a course regularly for God, you must be serving God through humanity on a daily basis. Your life right now is the sum of all the services you've been rendering to God through humanity.

Even Jesus was always on business.

'I must work the works of Him who sent Me while it is day; the night is coming when no one can work.'
John 9:4 NKJV.

In other words, Jesus was saying the work His Father gave Him was always burning with passion like fire in His heart. If Jesus can testify that He must be in His Father's business, how much more you and I? You must be consumed with passion to work for God. If the passion of service is not in you, then I make bold to say you are yet to truly discover your originality. You must be filled with fire for your God given assignment, you must always feel the passion to be a blessing to people around you.

If you are feeling it, glory to Jesus! Keep the fire aflame and burning. If you can't feel it, pray with me:

Lord, I want to start feeling the fire of your purpose burn in me every day. Help me to come to a place where I realise that nothing else matters in life more than bringing you glory and pleasing you with my life, in Jesus' name. Amen!

I believe in you.

DAY 17

BEWARE OF DISTRACTIONS

Recently, a friend's baby was holding onto his phone. We noticed he was slamming the phone to a table. So we thought, before he damages the phone, we should take it away from him. Every attempt to get the phone from him, he would scream and cry on top of his lungs and we would give it back.

After about two attempts, we decided to try an old trick - to distract the baby with something else, until he loses focus of the phone. So, we got one of his favourite toys, showed it to him, and before you could say, 'Jack,' he dropped the phone by himself without any drama.

This is exactly how the devil robs many children of God from the purpose of God for their lives. He gives them a distraction at the expense of their assignment. As soon as they set their sight on the distraction, they lose sight of their life's missions. You must know that distractions are not always bad or evil things. In fact, they are things you love and enjoy.

The devil will not try to distract you with something unpleasant or bad. It has to be 'the toy' you love and enjoy playing with. It was recorded in Genesis 3:6 NIV that when Eve '...saw that the fruit of the tree was good for food and pleasing to the eye, and also desirable for gaining wisdom, she took some and ate it...' You would agree with me that if the tree was unpleasant and ugly, Eve would not have taken it.

The devil still uses this old trick today, and it works most of the time. He distracts us with the very things we love and if we're not careful, we would have dropped all of God's mandate for us before realising we've lost our way.

This is a reminder for you to keep your focus on your mission, on your assignment, on your vision and what God has commissioned you to do.

In the words of my good friend, Dr Niyi Borire, 'Distractions are the wrong attractions vying for your attention.' You need to beware of the devil. Beware of distractions.

Apostle Peter warns us to '1 Peter 5:8 KJV:

'Be sober, be vigilant; because your adversary the devil, as a roaring lion, walketh about, seeking whom he may devour:'. - 1 Peter 5:8 KJV. Verse 9 then tells us what to do when we face distractions, 'Resist him [the devil], standing firm in the faith…'

Let me bring this home for you:

Distractions could be anything you love and enjoy.
It could be a great and well-paying job.
It could be a position in church.
It could be a new car.

It could be some new friends that are consistently trying to take your mind and time away from God.

You need to focus and hold on to what God has given to you. Most people are distracted, and they can't hold on to what God has given. So many men of God have lost their callings because they couldn't focus on what God has called them to do. Money, fame, material possessions have taken ministry and mandate away from some people.

Is it not sad to know that the devil is so tricky, and he is filled with subtlety? Yes, and believers should understand this because failure to understand will lead to more damages. Focus on your vision, focus on the gift and potential God gave to you, don't get distracted.

Be sober, be discerning, be vigilant. Don't be distracted. Focus on your mission. Focus on God's purpose for your life.

I believe in you.

DAY 18

EASY THINGS CAN BECOME DIFFICULT

It was my wife's birthday recently, and I took the family to one of our favourite restaurants for brunch. We ordered our food, and our boys ordered their favourite soft drinks.

Our eldest, Semiloore, ordered a drink that came in a bottle that had to be opened. Whereas his brother's was very easy to open. Semiloore's bottle looked like one of those ones that required a bottle opener. For some reason, that morning, I was not patient enough to ask one of the waiters for help.

I took matters into my own hands and tried to use two old methods I learned back in Nigeria while growing up. To use my teeth to open the bottle. I tried and that didn't work. I almost lost a tooth. My wife cautioned me. I also tried banging the bottle cork against the edge of the table.

Frustratingly, none of this worked. Guess what we had to do in the end? You guessed right, we called the waiter for help.

I was there thinking the waiter would bring a bottle opener. You won't believe it; she just twisted the bottle cork, and the bottle opened with ease. I nearly cried. It took just a simple twist.

Why am I sharing this with you?

Some things were not designed for you to sweat over. You just need the right tool, the right strategy, the right system, and the right method or framework.

God delights in revealing to us the right systems, structures, and strategies for our life's purpose. Like we had to ask the waiter, you may need to pray to God to give you the right strategies to deliver the vision and ideas He has given you. Do not think you can do it on your own. This kind of thinking would frustrate you.

You would see others around you doing it, and you would wonder why yours isn't working. Listen, easy things can become difficult if we don't allow God to reveal to us the right methods to make them work.

He holds the key; we just need to ask Him. Well, this can be traced to the reason a lot of people are struggling to get things done today, they left God behind and they were trying to do it their best ways. Well, I'm sorry to inform you that you

PURPOSE IS ABOUT DOING THE RIGHT THING

cannot get anything done in your own best way, you can only get it done in God's way.

You cannot force a round peg into a square hole, if you try it, it's either the peg gets destroyed or the hole gets distorted. You can only do it the way God wants you to do it. That's why you must not leave God out of the equation of your life, God must always be involved.

In fact, let me further tell you to stop doing things the way you've been doing them. Yes, I know it's the best strategy, I know it's the best and easiest way, but why not ask God for a more unique way of doing that same thing you've been doing. Stop trying to box God, you can't do it and be successful. Anyone who is trying to cage or box God will run out of ideas or strategies. If you want to go far in the journey of your life, then you must be ready to involve God in all you are doing. Keep God involved and He will make a big deal for you.

It may never have occurred to you as a prayer you can pray but you can ask God for the right strategies, systems, and structures for execution.

I believe in you.

Day 19
CONSULT THE WORD DAILY

Recently, we celebrated my eldest son's birthday, and it was amazing watching him interact with his friends, cutting his cake, and having great fun.

He received so many gifts, perhaps the most he's received on his birthday since he was born. One of the gifts he received was a tabletop football that we had to assemble by ourselves.

He brought it to me and said, 'Daddy, can you help me put this together, I can't wait to play it?' I obliged, thinking it was easy and straightforward. We began this thing and by the time we thought we were done, we realised we had missed an important element, and kept referring to the manual again, and again.

You know what I realised, each time we missed it, it was because we thought we knew what we had to do and failed to pay attention to the manual. It cost us each time because we had to unscrew it to correct a thing or two almost about three times.

Why am I sharing this with you?

Your life cannot be put together by your own cognitive ability alone. No matter how intellectual you are, you didn't make 'you' so you have to always consult your Maker.

If you try doing it all by your brilliance, you will miss a thing or two and they could be so vital to how your life turns out.

This is why God gave us His manual for life - the Bible.

We must consult it every day to know and live our life's purpose. No wonder Jesus said, "If you remain in me and my words remain in you, ask whatever you wish, and it will be done for you.' - John 15:7 NIV.

This is a key principle; we must let God's manual remain with us. It's not something we should check today and abandon tomorrow. In fact, God warns Joshua that he must not allow the book of the law to depart from his mouth.

'This Book of the Law shall not depart from your mouth, but you shall meditate in it day and night, that you may observe to do according to all that is written in it. For then you will make your way prosperous, and then you will have good success.'

Joshua 1:8 NKJV.

You know, the amazing part is that the Scripture is like a well and you can draw out any beautiful object from it. You can draw out success and prosperity from the Scripture, you can draw out leadership transformation from the Scripture, you can draw out your purpose from the Scripture, and so on. Don't ever think you don't need God's Word, you must meditate in it day and night, you must not allow it to get out of your body and soul.

Most of the people that won one or two battles in the Scripture are people who played the Scripture principle; talk about David, Joshua, and others, they all won by God's Word and its principles.

When Jesus was saying without me, you can do nothing, what do you think He was talking about?

'I am the vine, you are the branches. He who abides in Me, and I in him, bears much fruit; for without Me you can do nothing.'
John 15:5 NKJV.

Do you remember that Jesus Himself was the Word? So if He says, 'without me you can do nothing,' do you realise He is right to say so?

That is the truth, you can't do nothing without Him. You are useless without Him. You must do and live life with the Word of God daily, nothing can hold you ransom if God's Word has made you free. Be close with God's Word today and don't allow it to depart from your mouth.

Our lives must mirror the Word of God, day in, day out, if we are going to effectively fulfil God's purpose for our lives.

God is counting on you and me, and we must deliver.

I believe in you.

DAY 20

YOU HAVE AN ANOINTING

G od has given you an anointing to do the supernatural.

You may not feel like it every day, but the truth is that you are anointed. God has placed His hands upon your life and given you an anointing to carry out something supernatural, even in the midst of a very natural world.

You're not ordinary.

You're not random.

You are a vessel designed to express His grace, His power, and His wisdom in your generation.

Whatever God has called you to do, He has anointed you to do it. That calling may not look like what's on a pulpit or behind a microphone, but it is sacred all the same. It may be teaching, parenting, leading in business, serving in administration, working in healthcare, finance, tech, or ministry, the anointing of God is on you to do it well.

And this anointing doesn't come alone. It comes wrapped in wisdom, understanding, and knowledge. Scripture says: *'I have filled him with the Spirit of God, in wisdom, in understanding, in knowledge...'* (Exodus 31:3 NKJV). That means you're not just called, you're equipped supernaturally, even in things you were never formally taught.

Have you ever wondered how someone just *knows* what to do in their field or calling?

Or how they seem to carry a depth of insight far beyond formal training? That's not a coincidence. That's anointing. Some of us have a divine understanding of leadership, others carry revelation in finance, some are gifted in creativity, and for others, like me, it's in area of purpose. It's not something we sat in a classroom to learn; it was something heaven downloaded.

But here's the key: the anointing doesn't manifest fully unless you recognise it, honor it, and walk in it boldly. You can't keep downplaying what God has poured into you and expect to make a difference. The world needs your anointed voice, your anointed creativity, your anointed leadership. You're not like everyone else, and that's the point.

So today, shake off every lie that says you're not good enough or equipped enough.

PURPOSE IS ABOUT DOING THE RIGHT THING

Say this boldly: *I am anointed for this. I have wisdom, knowledge, and understanding for what I've been called to do. I will be an expression of God's grace in my world.*

DAY 21

CURSED WORK ISN'T WHAT GOD HAS IN MIND FOR YOU

I've been there. There was a time in my life when I was stuck in a job I absolutely dreaded. I stayed in it for two and a half years and trust me, every single day felt like a prison sentence. I would wake up with heaviness in my heart, drag myself to work, and come back home completely drained; physically, mentally, and emotionally.

What hurt the most was how it began to affect my family. I didn't realize it at first, but the stress and toxicity from work followed me home. I would snap, withdraw, or project my frustration onto my wife and children. Our marriage was shaky, not because we didn't love each other, but because I was carrying the weight of a job that was never meant for me.

Imagine being in an environment where your smile is interpreted as laziness. That was my reality. Smiling meant I 'had too much time on my hands,' so guess what they did? They'd give me even more work, just to punish the joy. That kind of atmosphere slowly chipped away at my confidence, peace, and passion. It was dark.

Maybe you're there right now; doing work that stifles you, makes you question your worth, and robs you of your peace. If that's you, I want to tell you: God never intended for you to be in cursed work. He wants to deliver you.

There is a kind of work that brings peace. There is a calling that fits you like a glove, that fuels your joy, and that aligns with heaven's blueprint for your life. But to find that, you must begin with purpose. You must ask: *God, what have You called me to do?*

Friend, God's desire is that you thrive in your work, not survive it. You don't have to stay stuck. There is more, so much more, and it begins with knowing His purpose for you.

You're not alone. I've been there. And by God's grace, I walked out of that dark place into light. You can too.

Day 22

WHAT DOES SUCCESS MEAN?

Some people will say; 'Dr Sam, you mentioned that success is not money. Let me get the money first, and then I'll decide whether that's true or not.'

But time and again, we see people who have wealth, popularity, influence, everything the world calls 'success' and yet, they're empty, depressed, anxious, and lost. Why? Because deep down, they know they've climbed a ladder that was leaning against the wrong wall.

In a world that equates success with fame, money, and accolades, this truth may sound radical: Success is not what the world says it is. Success, in God's eyes, is the discovery, attainment, and completion of His divine purpose for your life. Anything outside of that is failure.

PURPOSE IS ABOUT DOING THE RIGHT THING

You see, it's a futile pursuit to base your life on things that won't matter in eternity. Cars, houses, positions, and titles; none of them satisfy when purpose is absent. God doesn't measure success by what's in your bank account or on your résumé. He measures it by your obedience to His call for your life.

So let me say it again clearly:

Success is the discovery, the pursuit, and the completion of God's purpose for your life.

It starts with discovery, knowing what you were created for.

It moves to attainment, actively walking in that purpose.

And it ends in completion; finishing your race and hearing Him say, '*Well done.*'

You can be celebrated by the world and unknown in heaven. You can be popular on earth and irrelevant in the realm of purpose. That's not success. That's a distraction.

So, no matter what you have, if you haven't yet discovered what God created you to do, or you're not on the path to fulfilling it, then let this be your wake-up call. True success begins with purpose. And purpose begins with God.

DAY 23

YOU MAY FEEL UNQUALIFIED

So, God has asked you to teach people how to become rich and the first thing you did was look at your bank account and the devil suggests to you - what qualifies you?

You got the idea and are passionate about helping entrepreneurs get funding for their business but you haven't gotten a single one for yours and you're like, 'No way! I am not qualified.'

You have the passion for events and you can't possibly tell people about it because you haven't put together an event of great magnitude, so you feel unqualified. You have the vision to help young men and ladies get it right in their relationship yet you have never had any relationship nor have even had a successful one yet - and you're like, 'Will people even listen to me?'

Who told you that you must be qualified to do what God has given you the potential to do? Who told you that you must be qualified to heed the call on your life?

Last time I checked, many of the people God called and gave great ideas to were never qualified at the time of the call. God qualifies them Himself. God uses people based on His mandate for them, not based on how qualified they are. If you are waiting to be qualified before you start, you will be disqualified at the end of the day. God only wants you to take the first step and He will bless the rest of your steps.

You see, your first step into your purpose or mandate is like the first seed you are sowing, and if you refuse to sow that seed, you will lose the reward God is keeping for you. Stop waiting for approval before you do something worthwhile. In fact, I imagine why people will have to wait for approval from other people before they take a bold step. Those who wait for approval from other people will not get anywhere far in life because such people will not listen to the voice and leadings of the Holy Spirit, they will rather listen to the voice of men for approval at the expense of God's voice.

Here's my point: Stop waiting for man's qualification to carry out God's vision for your life. When you hear 'The Purpose Preacher,' you would think I have a Ph.D. in Purpose Discovery and Articulation, right? No, I don't! When God

PURPOSE IS ABOUT DOING THE RIGHT THING

asked me to do it, I had no qualifications whatsoever. In fact, at the time, I had only just begun walking in my own purpose.

But I was clear what He wanted me to do, and I was also clear He had given me all that I needed to do it. So, I started. When I did, I started to increase in knowledge. I read everything I could find on the subject of purpose. I wanted to know everything possible about it. I read books on purpose. I listened to audio tapes on purpose. I subscribed to podcasts on purpose. I followed people who also teach on purpose. Any preaching on purpose, I wanted to hear it. Any philosophy, any doctrine, any insight, I wanted it.

That's how I've been growing.

Hear this, for every purpose God has given you, He qualifies you, but you must grow in it. Your qualification is God's responsibility but your growth and value creation is your responsibility. Don't mix the two.

I love you. I believe in you.

DAY 24

GOD WANTS TO USE YOU. YES, YOU!

Imagine with me please. You are Moses. Yes, the Moses in the Bible.

Forty years ago, you thought you were passionate and hungry. You desperately wanted to save your people from oppression and slavery. You tried your best to kill one of the oppressors and imagined that your people would jump up in adulation. You expected them to sing your name and say something like, 'Our deliverer has arrived.'

None of that happened. Instead, the next day when you thought you could continue your deliverance mandate, one of them looked you in the eye and said to you, 'Who made you ruler and judge over us?'

You were so embarrassed. Like, 'Despite all am trying to do for these people, they don't even see anything in me.' You ran away to the wilderness feeling like a failure and murderer.

Forty years after, you were minding your business when suddenly a bush that was supposed to be burning failed to burn and the voice of God emerges from the bush saying, 'I am calling you to do that same thing you tried to do forty years ago, to the same people that rejected you.'

I don't know about you, but Moses' response would have been my response too, 'Who am I, that I should go to Pharaoh and bring the Israelites out of Egypt?'

Like, 'God, for real? Of all the people in the world, billions of us that You created, couldn't You find someone else to send on this errand other than an embarrassed failure like me who is now old and stricken in age?'

Like Moses, it is easy to look at ourselves and we see our past failures, lack of skill, our mistakes or limitations and we conclude for ourselves: I'm not the right person for this mandate. I don't have what it takes.

God's response is worth studying for days. He said, 'I will be with you. And this will be the sign to you that it is I who have sent you…'

Listen, it's natural to feel unworthy of God's call. It is absolutely normal. But what is not normal is for you to reject it. No matter how big, massive or grandeur it looks beyond your paycheque, self-esteem, or upbringing, what matters is that God has chosen you. Let me just tell you the fact here, many are called but few are chosen. To be chosen by God for His purpose is a great privilege you must not refuse.

I know you may be reading this, and you have a sense of God's calling on your life but you're wondering, 'Why me, Lord?'

That's the wrong question. Why not you?

God wants to use you. Yes, you! Stop wishing He was calling someone else. Stop wishing God would just leave you be. He is an intentional God. If He is calling you, it is because He has deposited so much in you to see you through the calling. He is with you and will be with you, so you are not, and would never be alone on the call. Feeling unworthy of that mandate on you is to think God doesn't know what He was doing for calling you.

The funny thing is that a lot of people ran from their calling and mandate when they were much younger, when they were in their 20s, 30s and 40s. They ran and ignored their calling until they were in their 60s and 70s. At that old age, it would have been so late because the energy and strength to go about for the Lord wouldn't be there anymore, though there is no doubt that these people would do God's work at that old age, but they wouldn't be able to do more, just because their age is telling on them. I want to challenge you to yield yourself to the calling of God today, He wants to use you. Do you know and believe that God will speak to people through different

PURPOSE IS ABOUT DOING THE RIGHT THING

sources just to confirm what He had been telling them over time? This is God speaking to you via today's devotion that you have a call of God upon your life and the best moment to start fulfilling that call is now.

You don't need to feel condemned because of your past errors and mistakes. You don't even need to feel bad because you messed up in the past and you put a lot of people in trouble. In fact, your family members may not even believe that you can be called by God but just believe in yourself and believe in God too. God is with you, and He will never forsake you to fulfil the call all alone. I trust God for one thing, if He calls people, He will always be there to show up for them. He won't leave and forsake them. The same applies to you, God won't leave or forsake you because He has chosen and wired you to do what He called you to do.

This reminds me of that song by Victoria Orenze that says,

'You'll never leave me
You said that You won't forsake me
You walk beside me
That is all that matters.'

Your sufficiency, competency and qualification are that God is with you, the moment this truth sinks into your mind, then you are set free forever. Even at your down and failing moment, God is still with you, when no one follows and believes in you, God so much believes in you, and He is giving

PURPOSE IS ABOUT DOING THE RIGHT THING

you backing. This should be your fortitude that God is with you, and that you are chosen by Him.

I believe in you.

Day 25

LAY ASIDE EVERY WEIGHT

Imagine with me the famous, highly decorated Olympian, Usain Bolt, in all his glory trying to run one of the toughest races of his life, say the highly coveted Olympic final. He then steps on the mark with a heavy load on his back.

The umpire calls the runners to begin their races, yet he fails to remove the bag off his back. Whereas on a normal day, he would be disqualified, let's assume he's allowed to run with the weight on his back. With all his talent, practice, strength and records in the past, he would fail woefully.

The reason he would fail is simple, that race was not designed to be run with a weight on his shoulders.

In the same vein, the race of life isn't something you can run with weights on your shoulders.

PURPOSE IS ABOUT DOING THE RIGHT THING

You have got to heed the advice of the scriptures that says, 'Therefore we also, since we are surrounded by so great a cloud of witnesses, let us lay aside every weight, and the sin which so easily ensnares us, and let us run with endurance the race that is set before us.' - Hebrews 12:1 NKJV.

Whereas it already would take endurance to run the race set before us, adding any other weight of any kind to it would just make matters worse. And no matter how talented, smart or strong you are, you just can't.

I have concluded that, as believers, we must continuously deal with things that clutter our lives. We must continue to declutter. Otherwise, we won't be able to effectively fulfil the purposes of God for our lives.

In the volume 1, I shared three questions you must ask yourself to declutter; let me share them again with you here:

Why do I have this in my life?

How is it adding value to my life?

Why should I keep holding on to it?

If you ask yourself those questions, you will begin to become intentional about decluttering your life. Always remember, only a decluttered life can travel lighter and faster.

Begin to lay aside everything holding you back from becoming all that God has created you to be from today - these include but not limited to: Besetting sin, addictions, unforgiveness, worry and anxiety, hypocrisy, pride, competition, selfish ambition, carnality or the love of the world, evil conscience, distractions, overwhelm, guilt, shame and reproach.

They all must go if you must fulfil your purpose. And you know, one of the tricks the devil would use against people so that they won't live a purposeful life is sin. There are people who intentionally enter the den of sin, they just love to put upon themselves heavy loads that keep drawing them back from where God is taking them. The truth is, when you keep on living in sin, then you will keep on carrying heavy loads and burdens upon yourself, you won't be able to move faster than you could, you will be delayed and retarded.

One of the many reasons a lot of people are experiencing stagnation and delay in their lives can be traced to the fact that many of them are going about with heavy loads behind them. I want to encourage you to let go of those heavy loads; let go of anger and bitterness. A bitter soul would not naturally find peace and solace in God. In fact, if at all you want to enjoy a sweet relationship with God, you need to let go of those heavy loads and keep your eyes focused on God. Don't be the same person delaying the manifestation of your progress, don't be deceived by the devil.

Lastly, discouragement can be one of the heavy burdens or loads the devil has been putting on you. You may be in a situation where you are not just encouraged to do something; you are not encouraged to go after your visions or dreams again, you are not encouraged to be around people, you are not encouraged to do anything worthwhile with your life anymore. Let me tell you something, you need to start encouraging yourself and stop pulling yourself back from the life God wants you to live. Start living in the reality of God for your life! Joseph could have been discouraged from pursuing the dreams he saw about himself, but despite all the ups and downs he encountered, despite the fact that he was hated and treated badly, he never got discouraged, he kept moving on, even though the journey seemed slow; he never allowed what he was going through to weigh him down.

Don't be discouraged as well; all the tantrum the devil is throwing at you now is just for you to get discouraged and quit. No, don't quit because Joseph never quit, he kept moving despite all the obstacles he was faced with. Show me a man that quit because of discouragement who got to the Promised Land. None! If you must get to your destination in life, you have to lay down the weight of discouragement and keep on moving, regardless of your circumstances.

I hope this gets you started on your journey to declutter your life.

I should also mention that it is important as a child of God to declutter your life at least once every 6 months. That means once every six months, you ask yourself those three questions and begin to lay aside every weight holding you back from running the race God has set before you.

PURPOSE IS ABOUT DOING THE RIGHT THING

I believe in you.

DAY 26

OBSCURITY IS NOT ALWAYS A CURSE

See, there are times God hides us away so we can grow and develop. He hides us away so we can remain humble while we're being groomed for His purpose. In the pathway of purpose, obscurity is inevitable - it's the hideaway that prepares us for our breakaway.

So, if it's looking like, no one is seeing your hard work now, no one is seeing the midnight oil you are burning, no one is seeing your sacrifices, no one knows the pain you are going through, no one understands your sleepless nights, no one sees the times you weep, no one sees the times you spend your last dime acquiring knowledge instead of 'enjoying' yourself, no one sees how committed you are, and you are not the star of the show now because you are always in the backroom; Hear this, it's only a phase.

This too shall pass. It's only a hideaway. You are being prepared for your breakaway. David was not a shepherd all his life. The shepherd phase was the hideaway that prepared him for his breakaway. Joseph was not a slave for too long. He eventually got his breakaway. Gideon did not hide in cowardice forever, God showed up and revealed his identity to him. John the Baptist was in the wilderness, but when his time came, people travelled from the city to the wilderness to hear him speak. Don't hate this phase of your life. Cherish it.

Don't curse it, enjoy it, don't quit it, rather persevere. Don't be depressed. Stay passionate, stay focused, stay on course, keep learning, keep growing.

Like David, while at it, chase the bear, pursue the lion. Kill them both. Gather your testimony. Keep growing your CV. The valley of Elah awaits you. Goliath will soon show up. Goliath must meet you ready. Just always keep it in your mind that tough times will never last, tough people will always do. What that means is that tough people will always see the end of their tough times. Be tough, be strong, be resilient and just continue to move in the right direction.

Imagine if David was not strong when he was in the wilderness, he would have given up not knowing that it's just for a moment. At the end of his trials and struggles, he eventually became the king. The reason you are going through your tough time is because you are a king, you are heading for the throne. The way to the throne won't be easy. Kingship is not for the fainthearted. You must be strong and tough. You must be like Joseph who despite all he went through became an overcomer. You must be like the three Hebrew men who were thrown into the fire, they came out victoriously. You will also come out victoriously, you have seen your struggles, and you will conquer and overcome.

Your days of obscurity are not days of condemnation, so don't condemn yourself, keep moving, and keep pushing. When it's time for God to announce you like He announced David and all the women in the town were singing his praise, the Lord will also announce you. When it was time for Joseph to be crowned as a prime minister, God did it without the consent of anyone. Even his brothers that were detesting him later came to bow to him. Let me tell you something, when it's time for God to announce you, no Jupiter can stop Him. Those who have been detesting you will later come to celebrate you and with you.

Remember this, it is the talents and passion you develop in the place of obscurity that God will use to announce you to the world. Don't quit!

I believe in you.

DAY 27

FIND YOUR DOMAIN

Life is a race, but it is not a race against anyone but yourself. One of life's major deceptions is to think you're here to compete with other people. You were not designed for competition; you were designed for dominion.

In God's dominion mandate, we're all made kings. We all have our territories, our own domains in which we're destined to reign as kings. When you find your territory, you find your dominion.

But when you don't, you compete for other people's territories, so you live your life based on 'survival of the fittest' instead of 'be fruitful, multiply and have dominion.'

The rules of life are simple, and they are:

PURPOSE IS ABOUT DOING THE RIGHT THING

1. Find your place (Domain).
2. Stay in your lane (Maintain your focus).
3. Run your race (Persistently and consistently).

As I always say, you only have grace for your race. Outside of your race and your lane, you will run wasted and frustrated because you will never have anything to show for a race that is not yours. God is counting on you to find your place, stay in your lane and run the race set before you with His grace.

That's why the Bible says: 'Therefore we also, since we are surrounded by so great a cloud of witnesses, let us lay aside every weight and the sin which so easily ensnares us, and let us run with endurance the race that is set before us.' - Hebrews 12:1 NKJV.

You can't run with weights and win your race. You can't run with bitterness, resentment and the spirit of competition and still win. The only person you are permitted to be in a competition with is 'You.' If you keep competing with other people, you will never get to your destination. Many people are like that today, they gave up because they think other people are doing better than them.

Competing with others will make you always see flaws in what you are doing. No matter how good you are, if you have a competitive spirit, you will never go farther. Your goal must be to see yourself and see what you can do to become a better person. You will never become better if you keep losing sight of yourself. Focus on who you are as a person, and you will get better as time goes by.

As you keep running your race and as you are focusing on yourself, make sure you also focus on God. Do you know why Lot's wife became a pillar of salt? She lost focus. When you lose focus, you will also lose energy, strength and rigor to move on with your race. Paul in Philippians 3:14 stated it clearly that he is pressing towards the mark of the high calling. It means, he is focusing on the prize that he wanted to win. Let me tell you this, there is a prize for you to win. If you lose sight of where you are going, then there won't be any prize for you at the end.

The key to your run is to fix your gaze on Jesus, 'Fixing our eyes on Jesus, the pioneer, and perfecter of faith. For the joy set before him, he endured the cross, scorning its shame, and sat down at the right hand of the throne of God.' Hebrews 12:2 NIV.

Jesus had to set his gaze on His prize to win, not on how anyone else around Him was running. Maintain your focus! Stay in your lane, eyes on the prize.

I believe in you.

DAY 28

TIME IS NOT MONEY

If time was money, everyone would earn the same per hour. Our earnings are different despite spending the same time working.

Value is money.

So, don't be busy trying to increase your hours of work. Do your best to increase your value. When your value goes up, you would work fewer hours and earn more than you ever did in your life. Increase your value by niching yourself and being known for something you know. This is how people and organisations will seek and pay you for what you know.

You would literally name your price, and they will pay. Please don't fall into the ' time is money' trap. Increase your value and watch you become sought-after. Sought-after people are people with great value. The degree of value you give will also equal the degree of money you get. You don't get much money because you are trying to spend more time on work.

Do you know that there are people who get $10k per hour, meanwhile there are people who get less than $1,000 per month as salary? It is not the hours spent in the place of work that matters, it is the degree of their value that makes them get that kind of money. When you eventually become a person of great value, then you will automatically become a wealthy person. Some people don't even care about the number of hours you spent on their work; they are only concerned about the value your time brought for them.

A company will pay the general manager a large sum of money, while the gate keeper will get just a peanut at the end of the day. In fact, the gateman may stay at the gate post all day long, while the general manager will only work for a few hours and go home. What's the difference here? Value. Yes, value. In fact, people won't even pay you because you have spent more time on a job and as a result you are sweating rigorously. They will rather increase your pay because of your rigorous value. You need to get this thing right and get yourself set free for a great life.

Meanwhile, I need to now make you understand that if you want to live a great life and have great value too, then you must be intentional living a purposeful life, you must be intentional about living to fulfil your potential. The potential of David brought him to the throne, the potential of Joseph brought him to the throne. Your potential can also set the ball rolling for you if you are ready to sign up for something serious. You can never truly live to the fullest of your potential if you don't know why you were created.

To not know the purpose of a thing is to deny that thing the full expression of its potential. I can guarantee that the life you are living now is nothing compared to what God has in mind for you.

The key to accessing all that God created you for is finding and fulfilling His purpose for your life. To live purposefully is to allow God to use you for His glory but not knowing your purpose is to allow men to misuse and abuse you.

Your life is more valuable to God than you can ever imagine. Don't let your years go to waste without knowing and fulfilling God's purpose for your life.

God is waiting for you. Heaven is counting on you and generations cannot wait to be blessed by all you've been given to bless this world with. Stop denying our generation all of God's deposits within you.

I believe in you.

DAY 29

FOCUS ON YOUR FOCUS

I was taking a walk around the Central Business District of Auckland (the city I live in) recently when I met an old friend. We haven't seen each other in ages. I was headed to a store to buy something for my wife when this happened. While we exchanged pleasantries, he said, 'If you're not doing anything, I am just going up the street, you can accompany me.'

He said those words whilst pointing in the opposite direction of where I was going.

I politely said to him, 'I'm sorry but I am headed somewhere else. In fact, I am going in the opposite direction.' We greeted each other and parted ways but as I continued walking, I began to reflect and made a realisation: The worst way to live life is to wander aimlessly through it.

See, if I didn't have a purpose and direction for where I was headed, my old friend would have taken me to where he was going. This is exactly how many people live their lives. They don't know where they are going and they are just tossed by every Tom, Dick, and Harry that comes their way.

If you don't know your purpose, if you don't have a vision, if you lack direction in life, other people will command your time, your freedom, and eventually your life. You will go where they go, do what they ask you to do, and eventually fit into their definition of who you should become. You are made to be who you are, and nothing must change that fact. The moment you allow other people to tell or dictate to you what you should be doing with your life and time, then you have started losing yourself or personality.

If you will lose anything in life, make sure you don't lose God and yourself. The moment these two are fixed, then you are in for a big shot. God has prepared a life for you, and He wants you to live that life. There is a template God has prepared before now for you and He just wants you to live your life within the confine of that template. The template of God for Joseph was to be a Prime minister, anything other than that is out of place for him. The moment Joseph recognised this, he remained glued to what God had been showing him.

Have you also seen the place you are heading? Then stay in lane, stay on track. People who don't know where you are going must not dictate to you how you should get along with that journey. Your journey in life is peculiar. If you have 3 or more friends, all of you must not head for the same course, it is not a crime if you all got split at a point in time so you can all fulfil God's dream for your lives.

If you are doing the business you are doing now because your friend is doing the same and he's successful in it, then you really need to sit down and check very well if that's what God wants you to do. I'm not saying you should quit the business, I'm only telling you to go back to God because His plans and dreams for your life may be bigger than what you are presently doing.

Find your purpose and stick to it, stop wandering like a bird that has no nest, stop going from one place to the other like a sheep without a shepherd. God is your shepherd, and He is ready to lead you on the right path, but He will only lead you if you give him the chance to do so.

The truth is you will lack your own identity, your journey will lack inspiration, and your ventures will be void of uniqueness if you want to fix yourself up for what others are doing. And, like a wandering cat, you will lose your way. Find your purpose today and let your life receive direction. Find your purpose today and discover your priorities.

I believe in you.

DAY 30

WHO IS IN YOUR CIRCLE?

One of the things that has helped me a lot in life is those I surround myself with.

Some years ago, I surrounded myself with people who had no idea about their purpose in life. So, none of our discussions had anything to do with purpose, making an impact, or pursuing the kingdom of God. We were always talking about becoming rich or making more money, getting a better or bigger job, and buying properties.

Now, my circle has changed. My friends consist of people we want to fulfil purpose together, win souls together, and pursue God's kingdom together. As a result, my motivation and drive for life have gotten better and I live every day charged up to fulfil my purpose.

PURPOSE IS ABOUT DOING THE RIGHT THING

Why am I sharing this with you?

If you want to do great things in life, surround yourself with others who are doing great things too. The people you consistently talk to, see and listen to will influence the direction of your life, whether you like it or not. What you are beholding consistently is what you will eventually become. The language you speak daily, you will soon become fluent at it. If it's the language of failures, you will soon be speaking fluent failure. If it's the language of success, you will soon become fluent at it.

When you surround yourself with great people, you either start to feel like you're not doing enough, your life is wasting away, or that you could do more. Trust me, those are great feelings, as long as they prompt you to action and not depression. If you have been feeling this way, now is the time to swing to action. Don't be ashamed to ask that friend of yours who is an achiever their secret to success.

When you ask them, please don't just be curious, be determined to apply whatever secret they share with you.

Those you surround yourself with determine your lot in life. If you surround yourself with the wrong set of people, everything will be wrong about you, while if you surround yourself with the right set of people, your life and everything will be right with you. Get new pals, get new friends, make sure they are already walking on the path of purpose, not those who are just wandering through life. Your circle determines what surrounds you. If you are in the wrong circles, you will keep running in circles without getting to a particular destination.

If you want to go far in life, try to get close to those who are already on the route of where you are going. These are people who will inspire and motivate you to do more, but if you keep moving with those who are not responsible, then sooner or later, you will become irresponsible. The popular English phrase says, 'Birds of the same feather flocks together.'

Don't make the mistake of thinking you don't want to offend people; that's why you are not parting ways with them. Don't make such a big mistake. If anyone is not seeing what you are seeing and if they are not going through your path, then depart from them. I'm not saying you should depart with fight and disagreement, just do it with wisdom and gradually withdraw yourself from them till you depart totally. Not everyone should be your friend. Don't they are nice and kind, then they must be your friend. A nice and kind person may not be a wise person.

Hence, be careful of the relationships and circles of friends you keep. As you are reading this book, I want you to start filtering and shuffling your friends, if they are not supposed to be in your life, then let go of them. God wants the best for you, and He also wants you to keep the best friends as well. It's left for you to make a choice today. If you want to get to your destination faster and easier, then go to those who are already in the place you are going, and you will also get there.

PURPOSE IS ABOUT DOING THE RIGHT THING

See, success leaves clues. If you want to be successful, learn what successful people are doing, learn the principles, and begin to live by them. If you desire to be successful, check your friends or circle.

I believe in you.

www.ingramcontent.com/pod-product-compliance
Lightning Source LLC
LaVergne TN
LVHW091601060526
838200LV00036B/941